OCEANS ALIVE

Sea Turtles

by Ann Herriges

BLASTOFF!
2
READERS

BELLWETHER MEDIA • MINNEAPOLIS, MN

JUL 17 2007

Note to Librarians, Teachers, and Parents:

Blastoff! Readers are carefully developed by literacy experts and combine standards-based content with developmentally appropriate text.

Level 1 provides the most support through repetition of high-frequency words, light text, predictable sentence patterns, and strong visual support.

Level 2 offers early readers a bit more challenge through varied simple sentences, increased text load, and less repetition of high-frequency words.

Level 3 advances early-fluent readers toward fluency through increased text and concept load, less reliance on visuals, longer sentences, and more literary language.

Whichever book is right for your reader, Blastoff! Readers are the perfect books to build confidence and encourage a love of reading that will last a lifetime!

This edition first published in 2007 by Bellwether Media.

No part of this publication may be reproduced in whole or in part without written permission of the publisher. For information regarding permission, write to Bellwether Media Inc., Attention: Permissions Department, Post Office Box 1C, Minnetonka, MN 55345-9998.

Library of Congress Cataloging-in-Publication Data
Herriges, Ann.
  Sea turtles / by Ann Herriges.
    p. cm. – (Oceans alive!) (Blastoff! readers)
Summary: "Simple text and supportive images introduce beginning readers to sea turtles. Intended for students in kindergarten through third grade."
  Includes bibliographical references and index.
  ISBN-10: 1-60014-022-X (hardcover : alk. paper)
  ISBN-13: 978-1-60014-022-8 (hardcover : alk. paper)
  1. Sea turtles—Juvenile literature. I. Title. II. Series. III. Series: Blastoff! readers

QL666.C536H47 2007
597.92'8–dc22   2006000610

Text copyright © 2007 by Bellwether Media.
Printed in the United States of America.

Table of Contents

4

Sea turtles are **reptiles**.
They are **cold-blooded**
and have scaly skin.

Sea turtles live in warm
ocean waters.

Most sea turtles have a hard, bony shell.

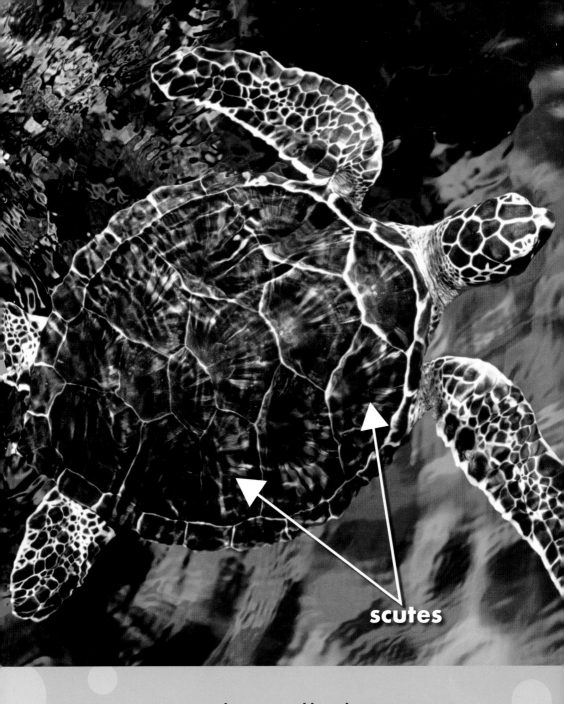

scutes

Large scales called **scutes** cover the top of the shell.

flippers

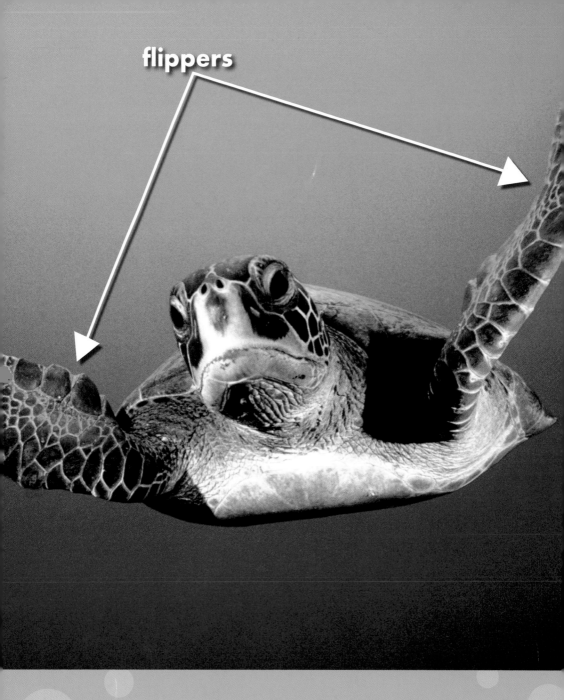

Sea turtles have four flippers. They use their front flippers to paddle.

8

They use the back flippers to turn and stop.

Sea turtles have strong jaws for biting and tearing food.

Most sea turtles eat **seaweed**, crabs, fish, and jellyfish.

Sea turtles **migrate** in late spring and summer. Females swim to beaches to lay eggs.

The female sea turtle drags
her heavy body onto
the beach.

She digs a nest in the sand
with her flippers.

She lays about 100 eggs
in the nest. The eggs are
round and soft.

15

The female sea turtle covers
the eggs with sand.

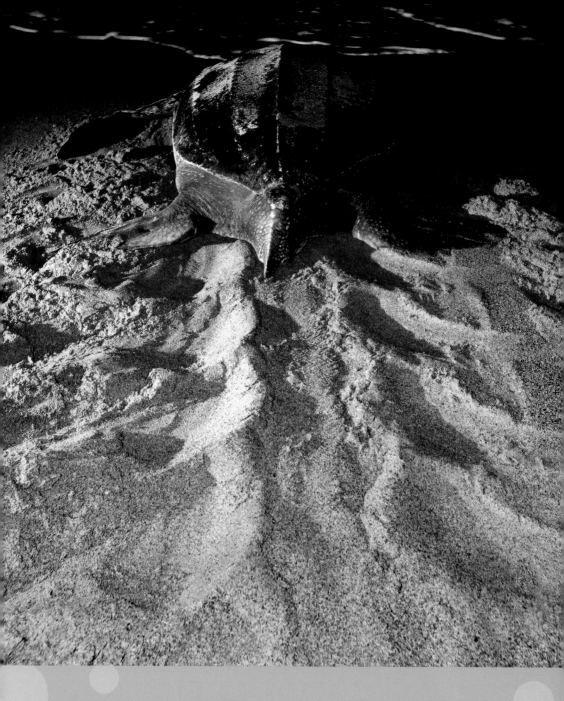

She crawls back to the ocean.

The baby turtles grow inside the eggs. They are ready to hatch in about two months.

18

The baby turtles use a sharp **egg tooth** to break open their shells.

The baby turtles dig up
through the sand and
scurry to the water.

They swim with the **current** and make the ocean their home.

Glossary

cold-blooded—animals that have a body temperature that changes with the temperature of their surroundings

current—the movement of water in the ocean; some currents are like rivers that flow through the ocean.

egg tooth—a small, sharp tooth that a baby sea turtle uses to break out of its egg; a sea turtle loses its egg tooth as it grows.

migrate—to move from one place to another; some sea turtles migrate more than 1,000 miles to nest; the female always goes back to the beach where she hatched.

reptile—a cold-blooded animal that has a backbone and lays eggs to produce young

scutes—pieces of hard skin that covers the top of a sea turtle's shell

seaweed—plants that grow in the sea; seaweed needs sunlight to make its own food.

To Learn More

AT THE LIBRARY

Andreae, Giles. *Commotion in the Ocean.* Wilton, Conn.: Tiger Tales, 2002.

Arnosky, Jim. *Turtle in the Sea.* New York: G.P. Putnam's Sons, 2002.

Guiberson, Brenda Z. *Into the Sea.* New York: Holt, 1996.

Pirotta, Saviour. *Turtle Bay.* New York: Farrar, Straus, and Giroux, 1997.

ON THE WEB

Learning more about sea turtles is as easy as 1, 2, 3.

1. Go to www.factsurfer.com

2. Enter "sea turtles" into search box.

3. Click the "Surf" button and you will see a list of related web sites.

With factsurfer.com, finding more information is just a click away.

Index

The photographs in this book are reproduced through the courtesy of: Georgette Douwma/Getty Images, front cover; David Fleetham/Getty Images, p. 4; Tim Laman/Getty Images, p. 5; A Witte/ C Mahaney/Getty Images, p. 6; John Giustina/Getty Images, p. 7; Douglas D. Siefert/Getty Images, p. 8; Steven Hunt/Getty Images, p. 9; Reinhard Dirscherl/ Alamy, pp. 10-11; Stephen Frink/Getty Images, p. 12; Tor Johnson/Alamy, p. 13; Cousteau Society/Getty Images, p. 14; Gerry Ellis/Getty Images, p. 15; Steve Winter/Getty Images, p. 16; Konrad Wothe/Getty Images, p. 17; Kelvin Aitkin/ Alamy, p. 18; Secret Sea Visions/Alamy, p. 19; Bill Curtsinger/Getty Images, p. 20; James D. Watt/Alamy, p. 21.

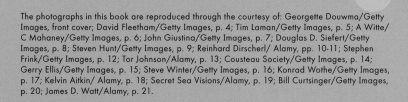